RAGGEDY ANN and ANDY
FIVE BIRTHDAY PARTIES IN A ROW

by Eileen Daly

illustrated by Mary S. McClain

GOLDEN PRESS • NEW YORK
Western Publishing Company, Inc.
Racine, Wisconsin

"Where is everybody?" Boy Doll asked Raggedy Ann, who was stirring something in a bowl.

"Hmm, let's see," Raggedy Ann answered. "I think they're getting ready for something especially nice to happen tomorrow—to *you*."

"To me!" exclaimed Boy Doll. "What is it?" He began to feel very excited.

Raggedy Ann smiled. "Wait and see," she said. "Tomorrow will be here soon." Then she whisked some pans into the oven.

The next morning, Raggedy Ann and Andy were up early. So was Boy Doll.

"What's going to happen today?" he asked them.

"You'll see—after lunch." Raggedy Ann laughed, and Raggedy Andy secretly slipped something very large behind the cupboard.

Boy Doll was so eager for lunchtime to be over that he ate only half of his peanut-butter-and-honey graham-cracker sandwich.

After-lunchtime at last! Raggedy Ann and Andy led Boy Doll to a corner of the nursery that was decorated for a party. The other dolls were gathered there.

"Surprise, Boy Doll!" they shouted. "It's a birthday party for you!"

Soldier Doll blew his horn. *Tooty-toot-toot TOOT TOOT!*

"Happy Birthday to you!" sang all the dolls.

"Why, it *is* my birthday!" Boy Doll exclaimed. "I forgot all about it—and no one reminded me."

The dolls laughed happily, and the party began.

First, Clown Doll showed them how to juggle three balls at the same time.

Then they played with the blocks, and they built a tower higher than Soldier Doll's hat.

Next they fished for prizes.

The last game was a peanut hunt. China Doll had put tiny faces and colored hats on the peanuts. They were fun to find.

Finally it was time for the chocolate and white birthday cake. Raggedy Andy led them to the table with a clapping march.

As Boy Doll was eating his third piece of cake, he said, "This is the most fun I've ever had."

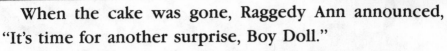

When the cake was gone, Raggedy Ann announced, "It's time for another surprise, Boy Doll."

"Look behind the cupboard," said Raggedy Andy.

Boy Doll rushed over to the cupboard, reached behind it, and brought out—

"A kite!" he cried. "A kite with a note on it!"

Sure enough! At the end of the long tail was a note saying: *Make a birthday wish, Boy Doll. We'll try to make it come true.* The note was signed by all the dolls.

"Be sure to wish for something we can give you," warned Clown Doll.

Boy Doll didn't have to think very long. "I want another birthday party tomorrow," he said. "And the next day, too. I want five birthday parties in a row!"

"Five parties!" exclaimed Raggedy Andy. "What—" He stopped when Raggedy Ann held her finger up to her lips.

Raggedy Ann took Boy Doll's hand. "That's a very unusual wish," she said, "but we'll try to make it come true."

The next day Raggedy Ann baked another birthday cake, a yellow one this time. Raggedy Andy thought up brand-new games to play, and the other dolls made two more kites because Boy Doll liked kites so much.

At his second-in-a-row birthday party, Boy Doll ate three big pieces of his yellow birthday cake.

"Isn't this *fun!*" Boy Doll exclaimed. He didn't notice that nobody answered.

On the third day, China Doll and Fireman Doll made two box kites for Boy Doll, and Raggedy Ann baked a pretty coconut cake.

Boy Doll ate two big pieces of this third-in-a-row birthday cake. "It's strange," he said. "I still like birthday cake, but I don't seem to like it *quite* as much as I used to."

The next morning, Boy Doll had no one to play with. "I wish I had someone to help fly my kites," he said.

"Sorry, Boy Doll," said Raggedy Andy. "I can't play with you until I think up some more games for your fourth-in-a-row birthday party."

Clown Doll and Soldier Doll were too busy to play, because they were making different kinds of kites.

Fireman Doll was putting up decorations. China Doll was setting the table, and Raggedy Ann was frosting the fourth-in-a-row birthday cake. Even Baby Doll was busy.

That day Boy Doll ate just one piece of cake, and the dolls gave him three more kites.

"What are you going to do with all your kites?" Raggedy Ann asked.

"W-e-l-l," said Boy Doll hesitantly. He was beginning to think that lots and lots of kites could be too many when there wasn't anyone to fly them with. But he didn't want to say so and hurt anyone's feelings.

On the morning of his fifth-in-a-row birthday party, Boy
Doll said to Raggedy Ann, "Please don't bake me any more
birthday cakes. They're delicious, but . . ."

Raggedy Ann put away the mixing bowl and cake pans.
"Maybe five birthday cakes in a row *are* too many," she
said to him.

Boy Doll hung his head. "Maybe *one birthday party* in
a row is enough," he said softly.

Raggedy Ann laughed and gave Boy Doll a big hug. "Maybe it is," she agreed.

"When will my real birthday come again?" he asked.

"Not for a long time," Raggedy Ann answered. "First comes Christmas, then Valentine's Day, and then Easter."

"That's good," said Boy Doll. "By then, I'll be ready for another birthday."

"I'm so glad I don't have to make up any more party games for a while," said Raggedy Andy. "What do you want to do instead?"

Boy Doll didn't have to think about that at all. "Let's all fly kites together!" he said.

Boy Doll gave Raggedy Ann and Raggedy Andy his two favorite kites.

He let each of the other dolls choose a kite, and that afternoon, all of the dolls happily flew kites together.

And instead of birthday cake, each of them enjoyed a big red apple.